WELL AGED

WELL AGED

CALIFORNIA WHISKEY AND SPIRITS
LABELS OF THE 1930s

Edited by Christopher Miya and Ashley Ingram
Foreword by Lance Winters
Introduction by Marie Silva

Heyday, Berkeley, California
California Historical Society, San Francisco, California

The labels reproduced in this book can be found in the California Historical Society's Kemble Collections on Western Printing and Publishing. Established through gifts from George Laban Harding, the Kemble Collections consist of more than four thousand volumes, extensive pamphlet and ephemeral materials, files of more than three hundred periodicals, and significant manuscript holdings, all pertaining to the history of printing and publishing, with special emphasis on California and the West. This book is published in conjunction with an exhibition featuring the Lehmann Printing wine, beer, and spirits labels at the California Historical Society, December 2016–January 2017.

Library of Congress Control Number: 2016946081

Cover and Interior Design: Ashley Ingram

This book was copublished with the California Historical Society. Orders, inquiries, and correspondence should be addressed to:
        Heyday
        P.O. Box 9145, Berkeley, CA 94709
        (510) 549-3564, Fax (510) 549-1889
        www.heydaybooks.com

Printed in Visalia, CA, by Jostens

10 9 8 7 6 5 4 3 2 1

CALIFORNIA
HISTORICAL
SOCIETY since 1871

VINTAGE LABELS
ART EXHIBITION

This book was published in conjunction with the California Historical Society's exhibition featuring vintage wine, beer, and spirits labels produced by the Lehmann Printing and Lithographing Company of San Francisco. Designed during the terrible privation and unrest of the Great Depression, Lehmann's labels invoke deliciously unrealistic fantasies of peace, plenty, and the high-class life and represent a forgotten high point of American commercial art.

WINE, BEER, AND SPIRITS LABELS FROM THE KEMBLE COLLECTIONS ON WESTERN PRINTING AND PUBLISHING

DECEMBER 8, 2016–APRIL 16, 2017

FOREWORD

Lance Winters

Product labels for spirits: they categorize, they give information, they make promises, they woo.

I design St. George Spirits's labels as invitations, as though
to a party. I need to give information about the party that the
bottle contains but also some idea about who's throwing the
party. I need first to captivate you long enough to inspire fur-
ther interest, and then make a pitch for why you should take the
bottle home. And if I want you to take a second bottle home
later, I have to make sure that the label hasn't made any promises that the contents can't deliver.

For me, working with old-school equipment like letterpress
machines allows me to more thoughtfully design labels. The
time that it takes to select type from a cabinet, arrange it in
the composing stick, and then lock it into the chase allows me
to sit with my concept more than modern equipment does. At
the end of the process, I either love what I've done or I throw
it all out.

What if you tried to go about it from the other direction
and imagine the tastes of the 1930s-era spirits associated with
the labels in this book? What can you guess about the long-
ago party if you only hold the invitation? I'm sure we could
come up with some fun hypotheses, but the fact of the matter
is that while many labels, including St. George's, are designed
by the same people who make the spirit being labeled, most
of the labels in this collection are from merchant bottlers or

people who bought bulk product from a distillery somewhere else and packaged it. These labels are therefore free from the constraints of any meaningful connection to the process or producer; instead, they reveal an idealized world of production or consumption.

This collection of labels is a magical trip back in time. These labels are aspirational, portraying fantastic worlds and exotic, far-off places. Many evoke the familiar lifestyles of top-quality bourbon drinkers with specific places and names. Look closely at some, and you'll see remnants of Prohibition-era text that showed malt whiskey as a medical prescription. In all of them you'll find the passions, preoccupations, and artistic styles of a time long gone.

INTRODUCTION

Marie Silva

Like many of life's sweetest pleasures, the vintage labels in this book were discovered in an unlikely place, tucked unassumingly between folders of more contemporary (and less captivating) wine labels collected for the California Historical Society in the 1970s and 1980s. Although the provenance of the collection was unknown, most of the Great Depression–era specimens— in their endlessly creative reworking of like design elements— clearly shared a common paternity. A little digging revealed that these exquisite labels were manufactured on an undeniably mass scale by one of the country's largest label plants, the now-forgotten Lehmann Printing and Lithographing Company of San Francisco. During a period of terrible privation and unrest, Lehmann's labels graced hundreds of thousands of bottles of mass-manufactured, highly alcoholic wines and liquors, invoking in brilliant color deliciously unrealistic fantasies of peace, plenty, and the high-class life. Marrying design with consumer ideology, the Lehmann oeuvre represents a forgotten high point of American commercial art.

The history of the Lehmann Printing and Lithographing Company is sadly underdocumented, surprisingly so given the firm's boasted success. Founded in 1911 by Adolph Lehmann with an initial investment of $190, the firm expanded into a major industrial printing operation valued at $600,000 by 1935. Referred to as "the printer who hasn't heard about the depression" by a dazzled correspondent for the *Inland Printer*,

Lehmann employed a staff of one hundred people, including a permanent staff of artists who designed each custom label with skillful care. Although Lehmann took personal responsibility for every label, it was his artists, toiling in anonymity and working overtime to fulfill an avalanche of orders, who assured that the Lehmann product met the highest standards of quality in concept, design, and execution. Lehmann seemed to interpret his own life story in Horatio Alger terms; after all, he was the son of German immigrants with only a grammar-school education who worked his way up from errand boy to become sole owner of an internationally renowned printing firm. Yet his labels tell another, surprising story: one of anonymous and collective effort coupled with endless and uncredited artistic innovation.

Although each Lehmann label is a marvel of design in its own right, the labels in this book are not "artisanal" in the contemporary sense. In today's artisanal culture, the individual creator is prominent, inscribing his or her personal identity on each unique, handcrafted product. In contrast, the stamps on Lehmann's labels remind us that these beautiful ephemera were mass produced, with figures of 50 and 75 representing lots of 50,000 and 75,000 labels. In 1934, orders from three large wineries totaled over $100,000 (nearly enough to cover the firm's annual payroll), a testament to the industrial scale on which both the wines and the labels were manufactured. To meet an ever-increasing demand for labels, Lehmann pioneered a stock label service in the mid-1930s, creating catalogs of generic labels with stock vignettes that could be applied to a wide variety of products. The inventive talent of the Lehmann art department continued to shine in the firm's extraordinary output of individualized labels, including the specimens that are found in this book. Yet even custom labels shared standard colors, backgrounds (parted curtains and aging manuscripts were favorites), and lettering.

We do not typically associate mass production with the finest craftsmanship, but it was within the context of high-pressure and anonymous factory work that the Lehmann art department flourished. Like John Ruskin's Gothic artisans, these unknown workers found in their daily grind an opportunity for seemingly inexhaustible creative invention. None of the labels is attributed to an identified artist; we do not know the size of the department or the names of the individual artists who constituted it. Yet each custom label order was treated individually—not as "cheap work," in Lehmann's words, but as a unique problem with a design solution to be worked out artistically. Lehmann artists worked with a somewhat limited visual vocabulary, conforming to and elaborating on a house style that is easy to recognize but hard to define. One notices the generous use of pinks, blacks, and golds; striking and colorful juxtapositions; and weirdly effective combinations of art deco design sensibility with faux mission, medieval, or antique vignettes. Characteristic of this style are the superlative Old Cathedral brand labels: modern cursive scripts and sans serif fonts are superimposed over the ominous image of a rising "old cathedral" that looks remarkably like an art deco skyscraper.

Lehmann believed that a good label was the expression of an idea, conceived and executed with a specific purpose. In his labels, these ideas were expressed in recurring motifs—the theater curtain and top hat; the chivalric knight and kindly friar; the heavy vine, peaceful field, and magnificent chateau;

the racehorse and yacht—whose purpose might be understood as the marketing of the California myth. A beautiful and unsettling example is the Varsity brand California Tokay label designed for Los Angeles's Hollenbeck Beverage Company. Two framed vignettes show a padre blessing a kneeling Indian and an oddly modern-looking mission complex. These appear against a classic Lehmann manuscript background, decorated with orderly fields and a plump cluster of grapes, on which the incongruously collegiate brand name, Varsity, is printed in ornate Gothic lettering. The label mythologizes both California's past and its present, illustrating a vision of racial and industrial harmony from which the bitter realities of history are excluded. (Old Dixie is similarly and wistfully invoked in whiskey labels that celebrate the idle comfort of the slaveholding class.) Again and again, as great strikes rocked both rural and urban California, Lehmann's artist workers turned to a romanticized past—the Middle Ages, the Mission Era, even the antebellum South—for inspiration. The beautiful images they created give us pleasure and give us pause. As I admire the extraordinary artistry and inventiveness of the Lehmann product, I also wonder: what contradictions lie in the glittering gadgets of our own design-driven age?

WHISKEY

WOODLAWN

25

WHISKEY

AGED IN WOOD

— ◦ —

RIO VISTA WINE CO.

DISTRIBUTORS

488-7ᵀᴴ ST.   PHONE LAKESIDE 1946.

OAKLAND, CALIF.

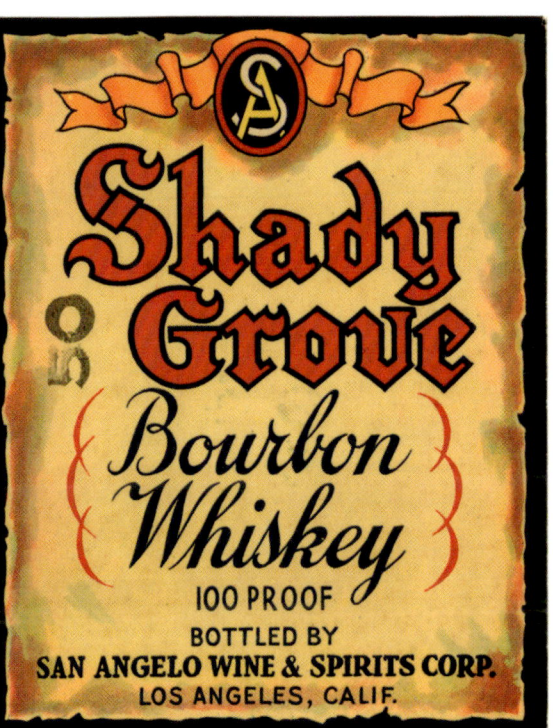

Shady Grove
Bourbon Whiskey

100 PROOF

BOTTLED BY
SAN ANGELO WINE & SPIRITS CORP.
LOS ANGELES, CALIF.

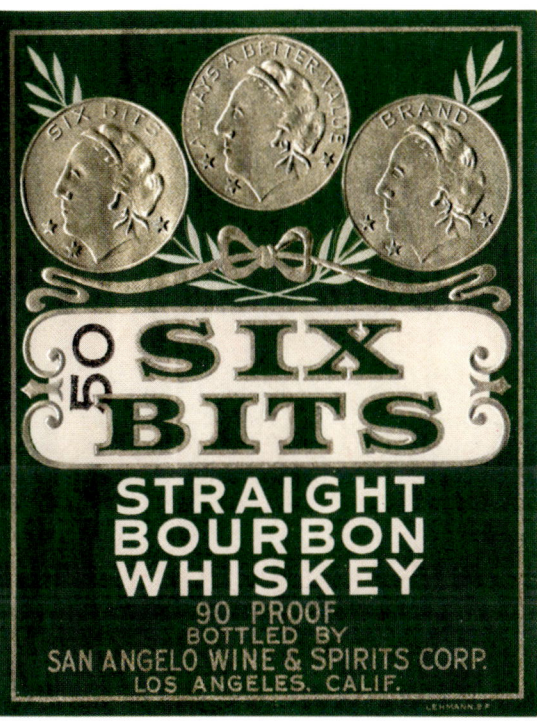

80 PROOF

YANKEE CLIPPER

BOURBON WHISKEY

25

BOTTLED BY
SAN ANGELO WINE & SPIRITS CORP.
LOS ANGELES, CALIF

VD

STRAIGHT

80 PROOF

UNION BOY

WHISKEY

BOTTLED BY
VAN DEUSEN, INC.
SAN FRANCISCO, CALIF.

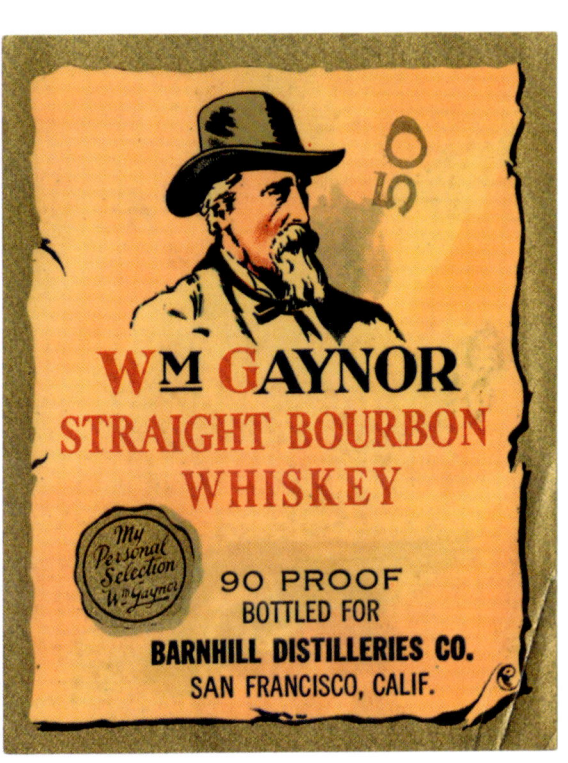

OLD HERMIT

BRAND

50

Aged
in
Wood

Mild
and
Mellow

STRAIGHT
WHISKEY

100 PROOF

REO DISTILLERS, INCORPORATED

NET CONTENTS 23/52 OF A QUART

KENTUCKY
STRAIGHT SOUR MASH
PILOT OAK
100 PROOF
WHISKEY
PILOT OAK
R. L. DALEY
PACIFIC COAST DISTRIBUTORS
SAN FRANCISCO
LOS ANGELES

BEST BET

86 PROOF  BRAND

Even money

Straight Bourbon Whiskey 75

BOTTLED BY
QUALITY DISTILLERS, INC
LOS ANGELES, CALIFORNIA

LEHMANN, S. F.

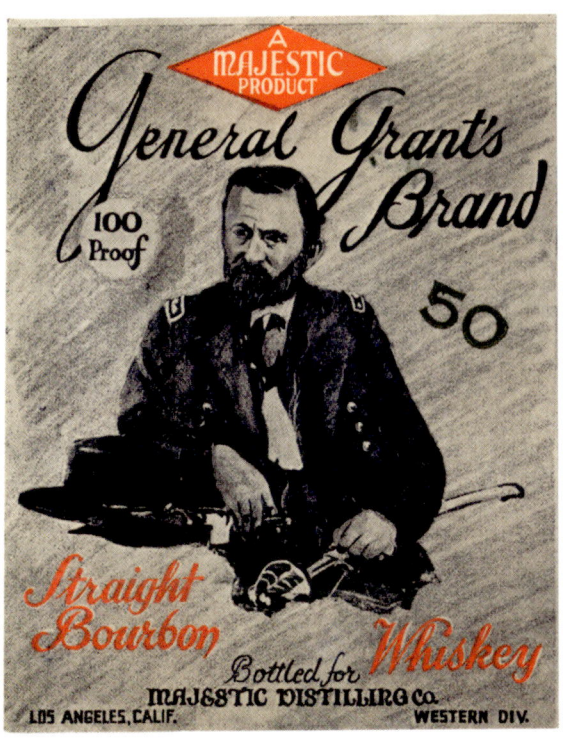

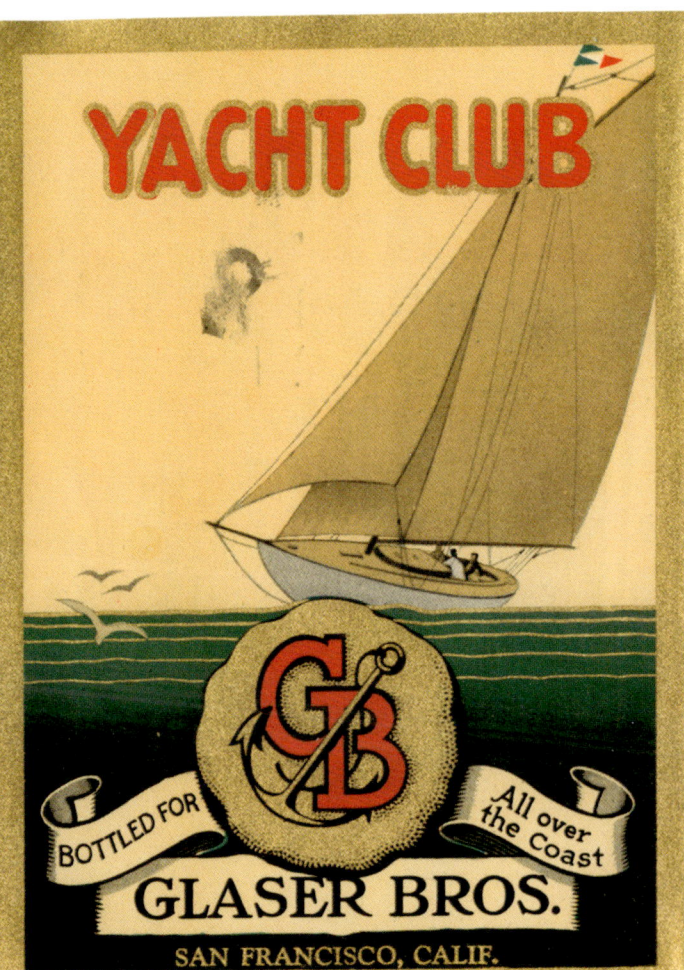

DEL
MONTE
SPECIAL
BLENDED
WHISKEY

BOTTLED BY DEL MONTE BOUFFET
BAKERSFIELD, CAL.

NET CONTENTS 10 OZ.

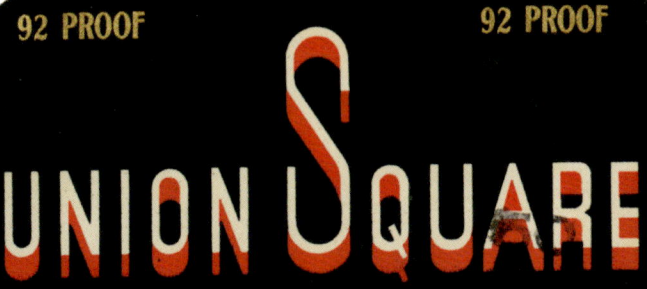

92 PROOF

92 PROOF

UNION SQUARE

A Blend of
Straight Bourbon Whiskeys
The Straight Whiskeys in this product are
six years or more old.

BOTTLED BY
PACIFIC WINE AND SPIRITS COMPANY
SAN FRANCISCO, CALIFORNIA

J. C. H.

25

SOUR-MASH

BOURBON

—

SPECIAL

HASLAM'S

THIS
WHISKEY
GUARANTEED
STRAIGHT GOODS

DISTILLERS

Old Grand Dad Distillery Co.

Golden's

𝔒ld 𝔐ountain

CORN WHISKEY

25

A MOST PALATABLE, MILD AND
HONEST BEVERAGE, PRODUCED
BY HONEST SOUTHERN PEOPLE.

BOTTLED ONLY BY THE UNDERSIGNED AND GUARANTEED UNDER
THE PURE FOOD LAW, UNDER OUR OWN PRIVATE SERIAL NO. 30920

GOLDEN & COMPANY Inc.

SAN FRANCISCO, CAL.

Wildwood
Straight Bourbon
Whiskey

90 PROOF
BOTTLED FOR
J.C. MILLETT CO.
SAN FRANCISCO, CALIFORNIA

GLENWOOD

BRAND

STRAIGHT BOURBON

WHISKEY

90 PROOF

BOTTLED FOR

GLASER BROS.

SAN FRANCISCO, CALIF.

SILVER RIDGE

American

Straight Bourbon

Whiskey

85 PROOF

BOTTLED FOR
VALLEY OF THE MOON WINE & LIQUOR CO.
OAKLAND, CALIF.

Sutter Home

25

WHISKEY

A BLEND

Sutter Home
Wine and Distilling Co.
San Francisco, Cal.

THIS WHISKEY IS **2** YEARS OLD

BROOKSIDE

QUALITY

50

STRAIGHT BOURBON WHISKEY

90 PROOF

BOTTLED BY

Rathjen Bros. Inc.

SAN FRANCISCO, CALIF.

Hart's

50

80 PROOF

BOURBON
WHISKEY

BOTTLED BY
SAN ANGELO WINE & SPIRITS CORP.
LOS ANGELES, CALIFORNIA

THIS WHISKEY IS **4** YEARS OLD

OLD McARDLE
BRAND

50

KENTUCKY STRAIGHT
BOURBON WHISKEY

BOTTLED EXPRESSLY FOR

EHRMAN BROS., HORN & CO.

SAN FRANCISCO, CALIF.

100 PROOF   NET CONTENTS I PINT

HARTSDALE CLUB

H

35

BOURBON WHISKEY

BOTTLED IN BOND

PRODUCED BY D. K. WEISKOPF   DISTILLERY No 9   DISTRICT OF KENTUCKY

BOTTLED UNDER GOVERNMENT SUPERVISION
at General Bonded Warehouse No. 2
First District California   Permit Calif. P-2
by South End Warehouse Co., San Francisco, Calif.

FOR MEDICINAL PURPOSES ONLY
SALE OR USE FOR OTHER PURPOSES WILL
CAUSE HEAVY PENALTIES TO BE INFLICTED

B·R·B·

BOTTLED IN BOND

WHISKEY

FULL QUART

Bottled Exclusively For

Blue Ribbon Beer Company

San Francisco, Cal.

90 PROOF

CYRUS NOBLE

STRAIGHT

BOURBON WHISKEY

The original contents of this unbroken package include nothing but straight Whiskey, at drinking strength, distilled from fully ripened mature grains under the closest scientific control throughout the entire process of distillation.

BOTTLED BY

TERMINAL LIQUORS, LTD.

SAN FRANCISCO, CALIF.

Merry Boy

STRAIGHT BOURBON WHISKEY

85 PROOF

Prepared & Bottled for

GLASER BROS.
"ALL OVER THE COAST"

© 1934

Distillation Fall 1934   Net Contents Four-Fifths Quart

25

Lewis 66

Kentucky Straight Bourbon Whiskey

92 PROOF

BOTTLED FOR
A. B. GREENEWALD CO.
LOS ANGELES, CALIF.

Hi-Lo

Kentucky Straight Bourbon Whiskey

92 PROOF

BOTTLED FOR
A. B. GREENEWALD CO.
LOS ANGELES, CALIF.

25

GLENBROOK

100 | PROOF

STRAIGHT BOURBON
WHISKEY

BOTTLED UNDER U. S. GOVERNMENT SUPERVISION

DISTILLED BY **HEDGESIDE DISTILLERY CORP.** NAPA, CALIF.

BOTTLED FOR
CONSOLIDATED WINE & SPIRIT CORP.
LOS ANGELES, CALIF.

LEHMANN, S F

50

Old Acquaintance

100   PROOF
STRAIGHT BOURBON WHISKEY

BOTTLED UNDER U. S. GOVERNMENT SUPERVISION

DISTILLED BY **HEDGESIDE DISTILLERY CORP.** NAPA, CALIF.

BOTTLED FOR
CONSOLIDATED WINE & SPIRIT CORP.
LOS ANGELES, CALIF.

50

LEHMANN, S.F.

BROOKCOVE

No. **5**

STRAIGHT BOURBON WHISKEY

25

80 PROOF

BOTTLED FOR
STANDARD DISTRIBUTING CO.
SACRAMENTO, CALIF.

Great Western Special

FULL QUART

WHISKEY

AGED IN WOOD

RESERVE STOCK 25

GREAT WESTERN MERCANTILE CO., INC.

SAN FRANCISCO, CAL.

HOME DALE

WHISKEY

A BLEND

FULL QUART

25

Bottled Exclusively For

Blue Ribbon Beer Company

San Francisco, Cal.

GIN

HART'S

SLOE GIN

BLENDED AND BOTTLED BY
THE ALFRED HART DISTILLERIES, INC.
LOS ANGELES CALIFORNIA

Old Tavern

Brand

90 PROOF

DRY

DISTILLED GIN

Made by
UNIVERSAL DISTILLERS, INC.
LOS ANGELES, CALIFORNIA

LEHMANN S F.

PIPER'S

90   PROOF

50

DISTILLED LONDON DRY GIN

DISTILLED FROM 100% AMERICAN
GRAIN NEUTRAL SPIRITS

DISTILLED AND BOTTLED BY

WORLD IMPORTERS INC.

SAN FRANCISCO   CALIFORNIA

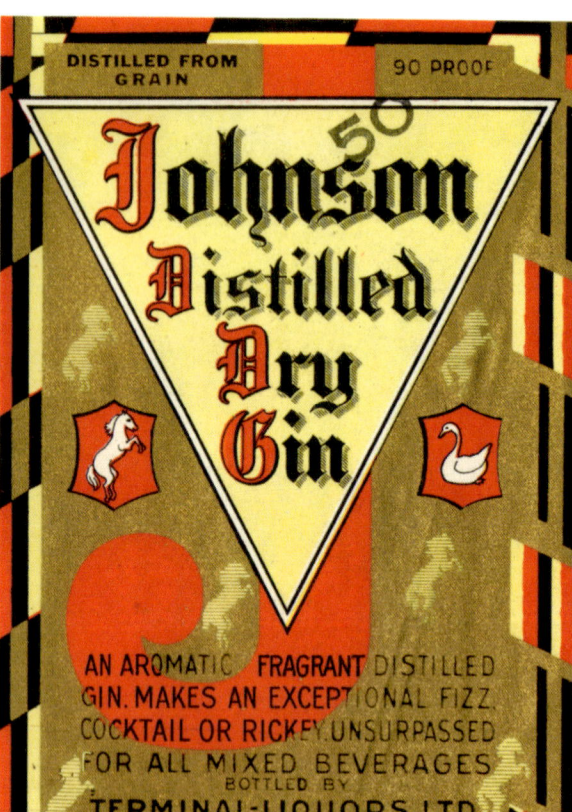

DRY
GIN

EMBOTELLADO PAR
E. CARRILLO
REG B-3   MEXICALI, B.C.

25

LONE EAGLE

DISTILLED
(25) **GIN**

80 PROOF

Bottled By
United Beverage Co., Inc.
SAN FRANCISCO, CALIFORNIA.

NET CONTENTS ONE PINT NINE FLUID OZS

Green Stripe

LONDON

Dry Gin

50

SHERWOOD CO.
SAN FRANCISCO, CAL.
SOLE AGENTS AND DISTRIBUTORS
MANUFACTURED BY AMERICAN DISTILLERS CORPORATION
ALCOHOL 45% BY VOLUME

PRODUCT OF DISTILLATION

RICHARDSON'S

NON ALCOHOLIC

LONDON DRY

TRIPLE REFINED

25

CONTENTS 1 PT. 10 FLUID OUNCES

PRIMA VISTA COMPANY

NEW YORK - SAN FRANCISCO

CONTAINS 1-10 OF 1% BENZOATE OF SODA

RUM

HART'S

RUM
AND
BRANDY

PREPARED AND BOTTLED BY
THE ALFRED HART DISTILLERIES, INC.
LOS ANGELES, CALIFORNIA

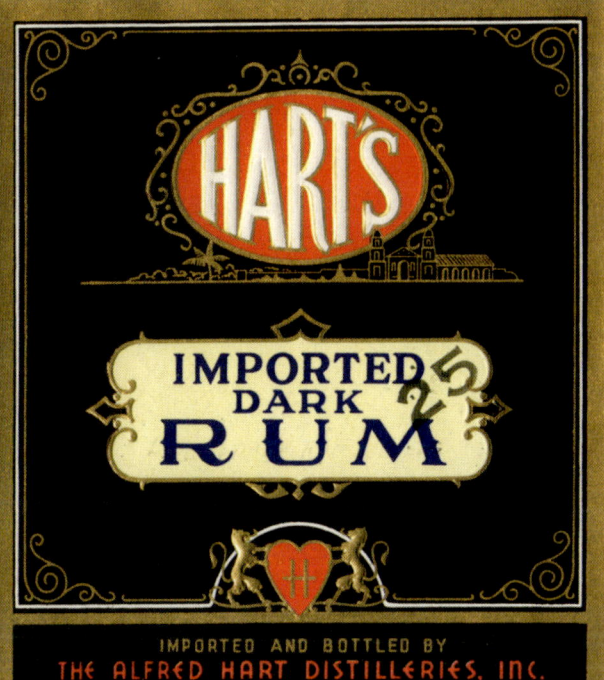

NET CONTENTS
ONE PINT
9 FLUID OZS.

FEDERAL
PERMIT
CAL. NO.-0-19

Old Buccaneer

25

TRADE MARK

JAMAICA TYPE
RUM

(90 PROOF)

SILVER SWAN LIQUOR CORP.
SAN FRANCISCO, CALIFORNIA

FERN

BRAND

50

ARTHUR FERNBERG

PRODUCER

SAN FRANCISCO   CALIFORNIA

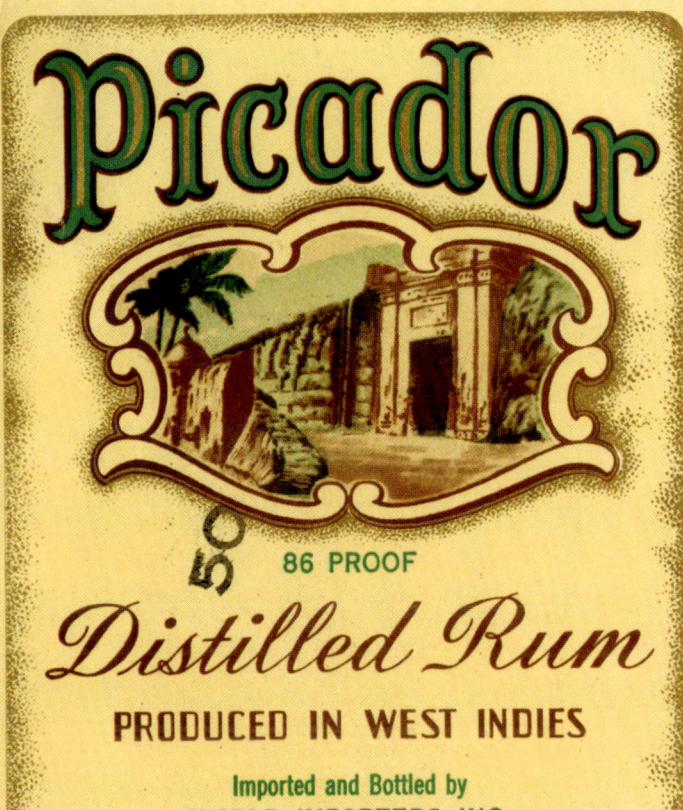

Picador

86 PROOF

Distilled Rum

PRODUCED IN WEST INDIES

Imported and Bottled by
WORLD IMPORTERS, INC.
SAN FRANCISCO, CALIF.

VODKA

HART'S

25

VODKA

PREPARED AND BOTTLED BY
THE ALFRED HART DISTILLERIES, INC.
LOS ANGELES, CALIFORNIA

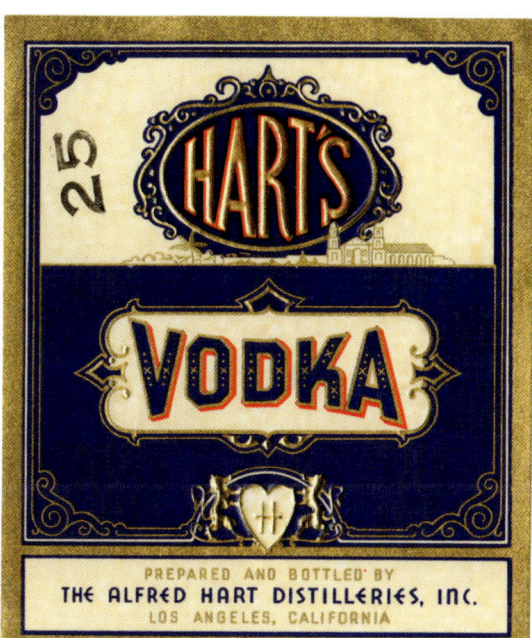

Miscellaneous Spirits

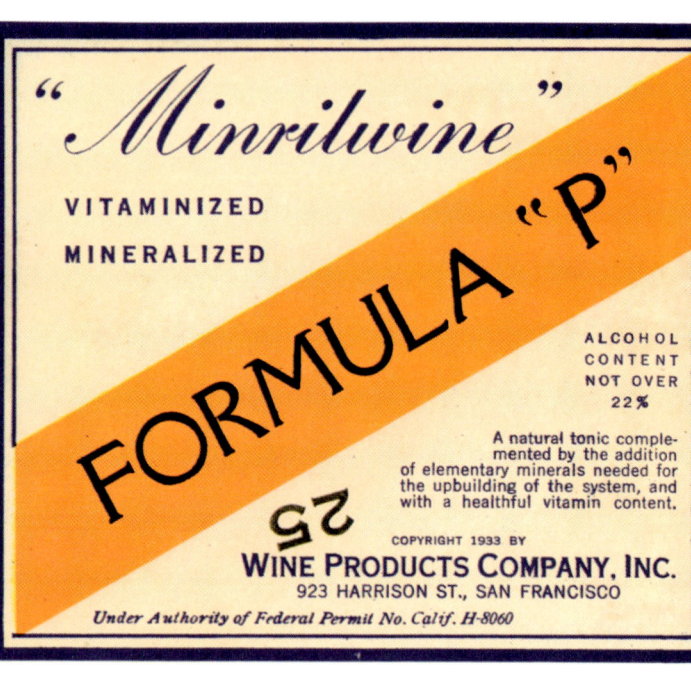

PEP-TOL

75

PEP-TOL

PORT WINE TONIC

PORT WINE TONIC

ALCOHOL NOT OVER 22%

MANUFACTURED UNDER PROHIBITION BUREAU PERMIT NO. CAL. R. 10293

© 1927

A RECONSTRUCTIVE TONIC AND BODY BUILDER
Dose: WINEGLASSFUL WITH MEALS
La Ray Pharmacal Laboratory — Los Angeles

PROOF

Bo-Kay

**APRICOT
LIQUEUR**

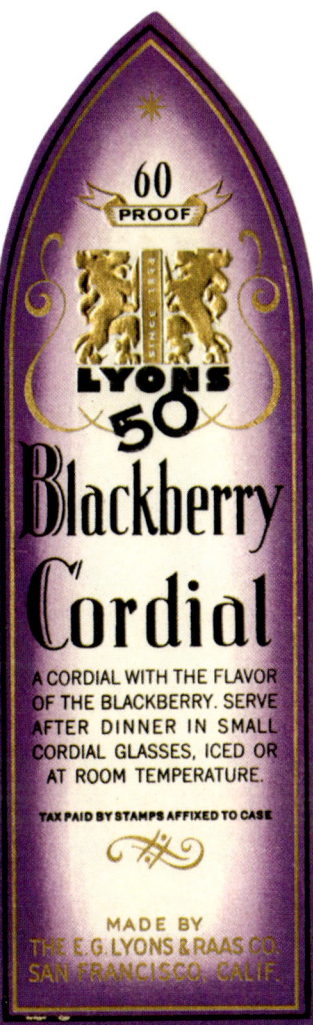

60 PROOF

LYONS 50

Blackberry
Cordial

A CORDIAL WITH THE FLAVOR
OF THE BLACKBERRY. SERVE
AFTER DINNER IN SMALL
CORDIAL GLASSES, ICED OR
AT ROOM TEMPERATURE.

TAX PAID BY STAMPS AFFIXED TO CASE

MADE BY
THE E.G. LYONS & RAAS CO.
SAN FRANCISCO, CALIF.

NET CONTENTS I PINT 7 FL. OUNCES

TRADE MARK

50

PRIMA VISTA

NON-ALCOHOLIC

APRICOT CORDIAL

QUALITY UNEXCELLED

PRIMA VISTA COCKTAILS, CORDIALS AND SYRUPS
ARE ESPECIALLY PREPARED BY US FROM
OUR OWN FORMULA. ALL INGREDIENTS

GUARANTEED ABSOLUTELY PURE

ARTIFICIALLY COLORED . . . FRUIT ACID ADDED

PRIMA VISTA COMPANY

NEW YORK   SAN FRANCISCO

CONTAINS 1-10 OF 1% BENZOATE OF SODA

ONE PINT   NO. 110

CRESTA BLANCA

APRICOT
CORDIAL 25

ARTIFICIALLY COLORED AND FLAVORED

BENZOATE OF SODA 1/10 OF 1%

Cresta Blanca Company

SAN FRANCISCO   CALIFORNIA, U.S.A.

HOME OF AMERICA'S FINEST BRANDY

Vai Bros.

OLD RESERVE
BRAND
California 75
GRAPE BRANDY
84 PROOF
THIS BRANDY IS 4 YEARS OLD
DISTILLED AND BOTTLED BY
PADRE VINEYARD COMPANY
CUCAMONGA, CALIFORNIA
4/5 QUART   FOUNDED 1870

ASTI COLONY

BRAND

CALIFORNIA GRAPPA BRANDY

DISTILLED FROM GRAPE POMACE
BY

ITALIAN SWISS COLONY

ASTI, CALIFORNIA

LEHMANN, S.F.

80 PROOF

LYONS 50

APRICOT
FLAVORED
BRANDY

DISTILLED SPIRITS USED ARE 100% BRANDY

MADE BY

THE E. G. LYONS & RAAS CO.

SAN FRANCISCO   CALIFORNIA

TAX PAID BY STAMPS AFFIXED TO CASE

50

HART'S

GREEN
CREME *de* MENTHE

PREPARED AND BOTTLED BY
THE ALFRED HART DISTILLERIES, INC.
LOS ANGELES, CALIFORNIA

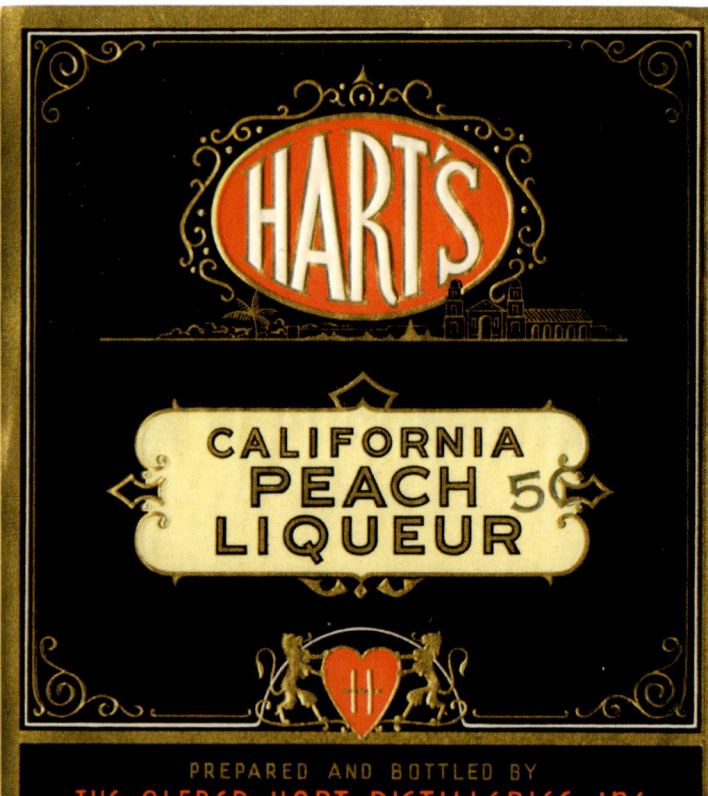

HART'S

CALIFORNIA
PEACH
LIQUEUR 5¢

PREPARED AND BOTTLED BY
THE ALFRED HART DISTILLERIES, INC.
LOS ANGELES, CALIFORNIA

HART'S

Kümmel 25

PREPARED AND BOTTLED BY
THE ALFRED HART DISTILLERIES, INC.
LOS ANGELES, CALIFORNIA

J.B. CELLA
BRAND

ESTAB. 1890

California

BRANDY

50

BOTTLED BY
ROMA WINE COMPANY, INC.
FRESNO, CALIFORNIA

⁵⁰ROMA

CALIFORNIA
BRANDY
84 PROOF
★

DISTILLED AND BOTTLED BY

Roma Wine Company, Inc.

FRESNO, CALIFORNIA

WINERIES · LODI, HEALDSBURG AND FRESNO, CALIF. · CHICAGO, ILL. · NEW YORK, N. Y.

LEHMANN S.F.

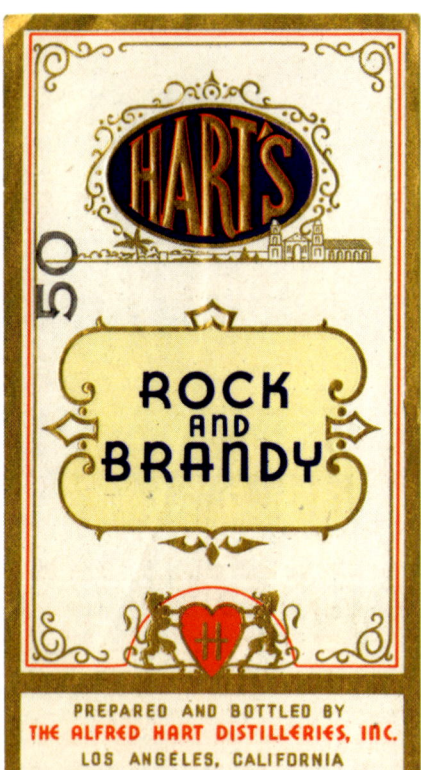

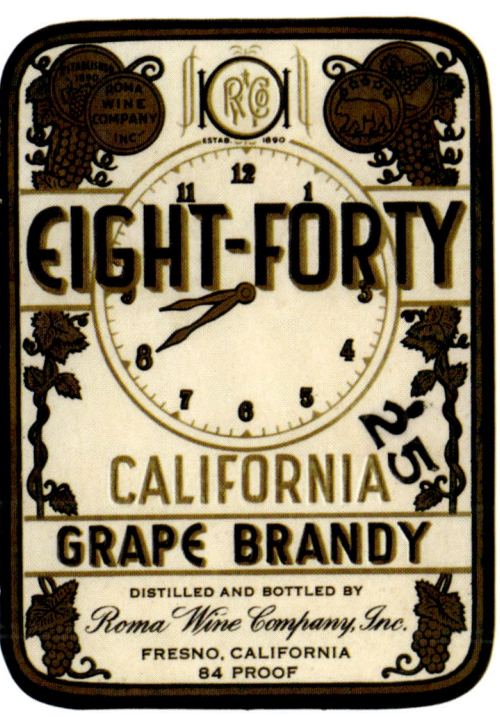

About the Authors

Christopher Miya is Sales Manager at Heyday, where he has worked since 2013. He can be found most days in his adopted home of Oakland, California.

Ashley Ingram is a lifelong Bay Arean who holds degrees from the Design Institute of San Diego and The Art Institute of California at San Francisco. She has worked as a designer at Heyday since 2013.

Marie Silva has served as Archivist and Manuscripts Librarian at the California Historical Society since 2011.

Lance Winters is the Master Distiller at St. George Spirits.

CALIFORNIA
HISTORICAL
SOCIETY since 1871

About the California Historical Society

Founded in 1871, the California Historical Society (CHS) is a nonprofit organization with a mission to inspire and empower people to make California's richly diverse past a meaningful part of their contemporary lives.

Public Engagement

Through high-quality public history exhibitions, public programs, research, preservation, advocacy, and digital storytelling, CHS keeps history alive through extensive public engagement. In opening the very heart of the organization—our vast and diverse collection—to ever wider audiences, we invite meaning, encourage exchange, and enrich understanding.

CHS Collections

CHS holds one of the state's top historical collections, revealing California's social, cultural, economic, and political history and development—including some of the most cherished and valuable documents and images of California's past. From our headquarters in San Francisco to the University of Southern California and the Autry Museum of the American West in Los Angeles, we hold millions of items in trust for the people of California.

Library and Research

Open to the public and free of charge, our North Baker Research Library is a place where researchers literally hold history in their hands. Whether you're a scholar or are simply interested in learning about the history of your neighborhood, city, or community, you have hands-on access to the rich history of our state.

Publications

From our first book publication in 1874, to our ninety-year history as publisher of the *California History* journal, to the establishment of the annual California Historical Society Book Award in 2013, CHS publications examine the ongoing dialogue between the past and the present. Our print and digital publications reach beyond purely historical narrative to connect Californians to their state, region, nation, and the world in innovative and thought-provoking ways.

Support

Over the years, the generosity and commitment of foundations, corporations, cultural and educational institutions, and private donors and members have supported CHS's work throughout the state.

Learn More

www.californiahistoricalsociety.com

HEYDAY

into California

About Heyday

Heyday is an independent, nonprofit publisher and unique cultural institution. We promote widespread awareness and celebration of California's many cultures, landscapes, and boundary-breaking ideas. Through our well-crafted books, public events, and innovative outreach programs we are building a vibrant community of readers, writers, and thinkers.

Thank You

It takes the collective effort of many to create a thriving literary culture. We are thankful to all the thoughtful people we have the privilege to engage with. Cheers to our writers, artists, editors, storytellers, designers, printers, bookstores, critics, cultural organizations, readers, and book lovers everywhere!

We are especially grateful for the generous funding we've received for our publications and programs during the past year from foundations and hundreds of individual donors. Major supporters include:

Advocates for Indigenous California Language Survival; Anonymous (3); Judith and Phillip Auth; Carrie Avery and Jon Tigar; Judy Avery; Dr. Carol Baird and Alan Harper; Paul Bancroft III; Richard and Rickie Ann Baum; BayTree Fund; S. D. Bechtel, Jr. Foundation; Jean and Fred Berensmeier; Joan Berman and Philip Gerstner; Nancy Bertelsen; Barbara Boucke; Beatrice Bowles; Jamie and Philip Bowles; John Briscoe; David Brower Center; Lewis and Sheana Butler; Helen Cagampang; California Historical Society; California Rice Commission; California State Parks Foundation; California Wildlife Foundation/California Oaks; The Campbell Foundation; Joanne Campbell; Candelaria Fund; John and Nancy Cassidy Family Foundation; James and Margaret Chapin; Graham Chisholm; The Christensen Fund; Jon Christensen; Cynthia Clarke; Lawrence Crooks; Community Futures Collective; Lauren and Alan Dachs; Nik Dehejia; Topher Delaney; Chris Desser and Kirk Marckwald; Lokelani Devone and Annette Brand; J.K. Dineen; Frances Dinkelspiel and Gary Wayne; The Roy & Patricia Disney Family Foundation; Tim Disney; Doune Trust; The Durfee Foundation; Michael Eaton and Charity Kenyon; Endangered Habitats League; Marilee Enge and George Frost; Richard and Gretchen Evans; Megan Fletcher; Friends of the Roseville Public Library; Furthur Foundation; John Gage and Linda Schacht; Wallace Alexander Gerbode Foundation; Patrick Golden; Dr. Erica and Barry Goode; Wanda Lee Graves and Stephen Duscha; Walter & Elise Haas Fund; Coke and James Hallowell; Theresa Harlan; Cindy Heitzman; Carla Hills and Frank LaPena;

GETTING INVOLVED

To learn more about our publications, events and other ways you can participate, please visit www.heydaybooks.com.